The **Essential** Buyer's Guide
BSA
350, 441 & 500
SINGLES

Unit Construction Singles
C15, B25, C25, B40, B44 & B50
1958-1973

GW00724618

Your marque expert:
Peter Henshaw

VELOCE PUBLISHING
THE PUBLISHER OF FINE AUTOMOTIVE BOOKS

www.veloce.co.uk

First published in February 2015 by Veloce Publishing Limited, Veloce House, Parkway Farm Business Park, Middle Farm Way, Poundbury, Dorchester, Dorset, DT1 3AR, England.
Fax 01305 250479/email info@veloce.co.uk/web www.veloce.co.uk or www.velocebooks.com.
ISBN: 978-1-845847-56-2 UPC: 6-36847-04756-6
Readers with ideas for automotive books, or books on other transport or related hobby subjects, are invited to write to the editorial director of Veloce Publishing at the above address.
British Library Cataloguing in Publication Data – A catalogue record for this book is available from the British Library.
Typesetting, design and page make-up all by Veloce Publishing Ltd on Apple Mac. Printed in India by Replika Press.

Introduction
– the purpose of this book

Mention British classic bikes of the 1960s, and most will picture the Triumph Bonneville, or one of the other big twins built by Triumph, BSA, and Norton. These beefy machines had (and still have) speed, glamour, and most of the attention. But the BSA factory also turned out thousands of bread and butter bikes: simple four-stroke singles that acted as first bikes for countless learners, and (mostly) reliable day-to-day transport for many others.

This book is a straightforward, practical guide to buying one of these – a C15, C25, B25, B40, B44 or B50. It won't list the minutae of every model's specification year by year – there are excellent books listed at the end of this one that will do that – but hopefully it will help you avoid buying a dud.

BSA unit construction singles were hugely successful. About 140,000 were built over a 15-year production run, and they were exported all over the world. And, despite being originally designed as no-frills commuters, they also won a lot of races. Jeff Smith won the motocross World Championship in 1964 and 1965 on BSA singles, and improvements to the works bikes, such as a roller-bearing big-end and all-welded frame, found their way onto production machines.

That was all the more impressive, given the original C15's nature as a simple ride-to-work bike mustering just 15bhp. The 350cc B40 soon followed, offering more performance with little more weight, not to mention better forks and front brake. In military spec, detuned to 18bhp, the B40 would see service with several armed forces. In 1967 the C15 was replaced by the revvy, powerful, and flashier B25 Starfire: a bike on which many learners rode their first miles. Meanwhile, scrambles and motocross experience continued to feed through, aiding development of the 441cc B44 and final 500cc B50.

So there's a wide range of BSA singles to choose from, all of them good to ride and reasonably cheap to run. What more could you want of a classic bike?

Thanks go to Peter Hallowes, Peter Bovenizer, Maurice Marston, and Mike Larcombe, all of whom allowed me to photograph their BSAs. Also to CCM for the picture on page 16, and to Rod Hann of VMCC Dorset Section for his help.

BSA singles make for a simple and easy-to-live-with classic.

Over 10,000 of these bikes survive, so there are plenty to choose from.

Contents

Essential Buyer's Guide™ currency
At the time of publication a BG unit of currency "⬤" equals approximately
£1.00/US$1.61/Euro 1.24. Please adjust to suit current exchange rates.

1 Is it the right BSA for you?
– marriage guidance

Tall and short riders
These are relatively small bikes by modern standards, so six-footers might find a C15 cramped. The B50 is physically bigger, though.

Running costs
Good news here: BSA singles are economical, while spares are reasonably priced.

Maintenance
Make no mistake, any bike from this era needs more TLC and sympathy than modern machines. You'll need to change the oil every 1000 miles to maximise engine life, and just keep an eye open for things coming loose or going out of adjustment. Not a 'ride it, forget it' sort of bike.

Kick starting
A whole mythology surrounds the kickstarting of four-stroke singles, especially the bigger ones, but successful starting depends more on the right technique than muscular thighs.

Usability
Pretty good. These bikes are easy to ride, lightweight, and have good handling.

Like any classic, these BSAs need sympathetic ownership – but that's all part of the experience.

A C15 isn't really up to fast modern roads, and nor are its brakes. Keep off motorways, whichever model it is.

Parts availability
Excellent, with many parts still being made. You can't build up a new bike from new parts, but you should be able to find just about everything you need. Secondhand spares come up as well.

Parts costs
Again, pretty good. Because so many BSA singles were made and are still around (and some parts didn't change for years), spares aren't expensive.

Insurance group
Go for a classic bike limited mileage policy, such as that offered by Carole Nash or Footman James, and you won't pay much for insurance, either.

Investment potential
Limited, because over 10,000 BSA unit singles survive, and they still aren't as sought after as a Triumph or Norton.

Foibles
The clutch is a weak point, and they vibrate at high revs.

Plus points
Economical, relatively affordable classic that will not drop in value.

Minus points
Performance (and in some cases braking power) is limited by modern standards, and BSA singles arguably lack the glamour of bigger British bikes or the Triumph 350/500 twins.

Alternatives
If you want a British classic from the late 1950s/1960s, there are single-cylinder alternatives from AJS/Matchless, or the far rarer and more expensive Velocettes. The BSAs are much easier to find. For a different alternative to the C15, consider the Velocette LE (water-cooled flat-twin), or the two-stroke Ariel Arrow and its variants.

2 Cost considerations
– affordable, or a money pit?

The spares situation for BSA unit singles is very good, with many items available. Because of the number of BSAs around, some parts are being made new, and prices are reasonable. The prices below are from two BSA specialists, for the B25, though prices for other models will be similar.

Complete restoration (basket case to concours) – around ●x8000
Air filter element – ●x10
Alternator stator – ●x73
Brake shoes (front) – ●x27
Brake complete (7in TLS) – ●x227
Battery carrier – ●x27
Carburettor gasket set – ●x3
Clutch centre assembly – ●x81
Clutch friction plate (each) – ●x6
Crankshaft assembly – ●x170
Cylinder liner – ●x46
Downpipe (high-level) – ●x58
Electronic ignition (Boyer) – ●x91
Footrest rubbers (pair) – ●x9.50
Fork stanchions (pair) – ●x91
Fork seals (pair) – ●x6
Gasket set – ●x30
Gearbox mainshaft – ●x70
Ignition switch – ●x33
Mudguard (rear) – ●x102
Piston – ●x105.50
Primary chain – ●x36
Rear light (Lucas 679) – ●x14.50
Rear shocks (pair) – ●x65
Rear sprocket – ●x28
Seat – ●x204
Side panel (replica) – ●x27.50
Silencer – ●x80
Steering head bearing set – ●x41
Tachometer (1971-72) – ●x119
Tank badges (pair) – ●x36
Wiring loom – ●x59

Many spares are available new ...

... though some, like the missing timing cover on this B25SS, aren't.

3 Living with a BSA single
– will you get along together?

BSA unit singles are generally quite easy to live with. They are lightweight, easy to ride and handle well. They're also very economical (expect over 80mpg from a C15) and spares are easy to find. Although the smaller bikes are slow in modern traffic, and the bigger ones are trickier to start, these are not finicky thoroughbreds – they were designed for the average rider to use every day.

On the other hand, if you are new to classic British bikes, there is one thing to consider. We live in a world where consumer products keep working without much attention – it's an age in which bikes only need an oil check and chain tweak between dealer services – but old machines aren't like that, and BSA singles are no exception. There's no getting away from it: they do need more TLC than a modern bike.

This just doesn't involve maintenance, which needs to be frequent, with oil changes every 1000 miles. It's more of a mindset that comes with owning an older bike, a constant awareness of things coming loose or leaking, of catching minor problems before they turn into major ones. This is all part of classic bike ownership, and many owners would say it's part of what makes owning a BSA single (or indeed most old bikes) different from a bike that always starts on the button and never goes wrong.

Still smiling after 25 years of ownership ...

Later bikes had plenty of flash and glamour.

Talking of starting, this is another challenge of BSA ownership, if you've never had to kickstart before. In fact, starting a four-stroke single (with the possible exception of the high compression B50) is not a black art, and doesn't demand bulging muscles. The smaller, lower compression C15 and B40 in particular, are not difficult to kick into life. However, there is a technique (see page 35), and, when looking at a bike, ask the owner what works best for them. Once it is mastered, it's far more satisifying than just pressing a button.

The other good news is that there's a big community out there, with a huge resource of hard-won knowledge about BSAs, active owners clubs all over the

world, and several specialist parts suppliers who can advise on a particular problem. So you won't be on your own. Also, certain improvements will make the bike more reliable without taking away from originality: electronic ignition, a cartridge oil filter, and solid state regulator/ rectifier are the key ones, while early bikes with plain-bearing big-ends can be converted to roller bearings.

As mentioned in the introduction, there's a wide range of BSA singles, from the mild-mannered C15 to the more fearsome B50. Which one you choose really depends on your budget, and the sort of riding you want to do. The C15 is generally the cheapest to buy, and will give 80-100mpg, but its realistic cruising speed is only 45-50mph, and the 6in front brake isn't really up to modern cut and thrust traffic. It's fine for gentle riding on quieter roads, though.

The B40 is a different proposition, with reliable 50-55mph cruising and better brakes. Again, not a motorway machine (as none of these are), but perfectly capable of longer runs. The rare sports versions of these two bikes (SS80 and SS90 respectively) are faster on paper, but need to be worked hard to deliver. The same goes for the B25 Starfire, highly tuned by BSA in an attempt to attract teenage riders. A Starfire should give at least the same performance as a B40, with sparkier acceleration, but the more highly stressed engine has a reputation for a shorter life.

The biggest singles have, not surprisingly, the best performance, with the B44 able to cruise at 60-70mph, with far more relaxed power delivery than the B25. It still gives 60mpg (70-80mpg at lower speeds), and, like all these BSAs, feels small, slim, and light compared to a modern bike. If it's a 1969-70 machine with the twin-leading shoe front drum, it's got the best brake, as well. The B50, with its bigger capacity and higher compression, is slightly faster, though its main advantage is a stronger three-main-bearing end and improved breathing for oil tightness.

Of all these singles, the C15s, B40s and B25s are the most common secondhand, at least in the UK, followed by the B44. Far fewer 1971-72 B25s and B50s were made, which is reflected in their value now, especially the B50. If you like the idea of a real rarity, keep looking out for an original C15 Trials or Scrambles, but remember that many C15s have been home-converted to trials spec over the years. The SS80 and SS90 of the early '60s are other candidates, as is the 1969-71 Fleetstar.

Whichever BSA unit single you choose, it should prove a fun and fairly undemanding classic to own. And if the two of you don't get on, you shouldn't have a problem reselling, as they are always in demand.

4 Relative values
– which model for you?

See chapter 12 for value assessment. This chapter shows, in percentage terms, the value of individual models in good condition – we've taken the value of a typical B40 as our base line (100%). There were many variations on the BSA unit single theme over its long production life, and this chapter also looks at the strengths and weaknesses of each model, so that you can decide which is best for you. We've split the bikes into capacity classes: early 250s (C15); later 250s (C25, B25); 350s (B40); 441/500s (B44, B50), plus mentions of the Triumph-badged derivatives and CCMs.

Range availability

250cc Singles
1958-67	C15 250 Star
1959-65	C15T Trials
1959-65	C15S Scrambler
1961-65	C15 SS80 Sports Star
1966-67	C15 Sportsman
1967	C25 Barracuda
1968-70	B25S Starfire
1969-70	B25FS Fleetstar
1971-72	B25SS Gold Star
1971-72	B25T Victor Trail
1971-72	B25FS Fleetstar

Simplicity itself: the original 250cc C15.

350cc Singles
1961-65	B40 350 Star
1962-65	B40SS Sports Star
1967-70	B40 WD

441/500cc Singles
1965-67	B44 GP Scrambler
1966-68	B44VE Victor Enduro Trail
1967	B44VR Victor Roadster
1968-70	B44SS Shooting Star
1969-70	B44VS Victor Special Trail
1971-73	B50SS Gold Star
1971-73	B50T Victor Trail
1971-73	B50MX Victor Scrambler

The C15 isn't fast, but is easy to ride and very economical.

1958-66 C15 250cc singles
Today, the 250cc learner law has long gone, but these 250cc BSAs remain a good choice – easy to ride and good on fuel – as long as you accept the performance limitations.

The original C15 Star was launched

Many C15s have been converted to trials spec.

in late 1958 (for the '59 model year) as a replacement for the ageing C12, its biggest and most obvious advance being the move to unit construction, which looked cleaner and more modern, saved weight, and was cheaper to make. Back then, 250s were primarily seen as cheap, ride to work bikes, and the C15 was certainly designed as such, with simple 6-volt electrics and sensible heavily valanced mudguards. It was in a mild state of tune, with a 7.25:1 compression ratio and 15bhp at 7000rpm. The C15 wasn't fast, but with a top speed of 70mph and 45-50mph cruising, was lively enough for its day and offered 80-100mpg.

The basic commuter C15 was soon joined by Trials and Scrambles variants, forseeing a glorious competition history for the BSA singles. They had greater ground clearance and several other modifications, and from 1960 the Scrambles came in a slightly higher state of tune. Lights were optional, and ignition by energy transfer, as the C15T and S weren't intended as dual-purpose road legal trail bikes. Exceptions were the rare Trials Pastoral, and US market Trials Cat and Starfire Roadster. The competition C15s received a roller-bearing big-end in 1962, and all-welded frame in '63. Production ended in '65.

Another variant was the Sports Star 80, or SS80, offered from 1961 as a tuned-up C15 with more chrome and extra performance thanks to higher compression, bigger inlet valve, close-ratio gearbox and other changes. The '80' referred to the claimed top speed, and some magazine tests exceeded that.

Meanwhile, the basic C15 received the roller-bearing big-end for 1964, and contact breaker points moved from the 'distributor' to the timing case the following year. One model to look for is the C15 from the mid-'66 model year, with the stronger competition-derived bottom end with roller and ball-bearing main bearings – the engine prefix is C15G.

Strengths: Simple, economical, cheap to run
Weaknesses: Low performance, weak brakes
Value: C15 67%, SS80 103%

1967-71 C25/B25 250cc singles

The C15 was effectively replaced for 1967 by the C25 Barracuda and B25 Starfire (though it was still available in some markets). These two (the Barracuda for the UK and Starfire for the USA) were almost identical, but very different from the C15. By the late 1960s motorcyclists were getting younger, in love with speed, horsepower, and glamour. The C15 couldn't provide any of that, but the new 250s were on the button, restyled with more panache and claiming 25bhp, thanks to a 10:1 compression, big valves, and other changes.

Unfortunately, this overstressed the internals – BSA had reverted to a plain big-end, which needed a good supply of clean oil, something the crude filtration system and young maintenance-shy learner riders couldn't always manage. The new 250s were fast and revvy, with an 80mph top speed and a willingness to rev out to over 8000rpm, but this made bottom end failures even more likely.

On the plus side, the B25 (the C25

The highly-tuned B25 was aimed at power-hungry learner riders.

B25s have a poor reputation for engine life, though this one has survived well.

Final B25SS in need of TLC – whatever the condition, it's a rare bike.

tag was dropped after a year) had a strong and good handling all-welded frame, based on that of the competition C15s. This was backed up by more substantial forks, while the electrics were updated with a more reliable 12-volt Zener diode system.

Despite engine reliability shortcomings, there were few changes to the B25 Starfire in its three-year life, except to the brakes. A full-width front hub arrived for 1967, and '69 saw the BSA-Triumph twin-leading shoe brake added, which in 7in form was well up to the bike's performance. One variant on the B25 theme was the Fleetstar introduced for 1969: a lower compression Starfire (8.5:1 for 21bhp) aimed at fleet customers such as the police. It remained in production until 1971.

The final 250s were the 1971 B25SS Gold Star and B25T Victor Trail, with all-new frames, new brakes and new styling, along with the rest of the BSA/Triumph range that year. They looked very different, but the engine was largely unchanged, except for the big improvement of a full-flow paper oil filter, and slightly less claimed power at 22.5bhp. Ceriani-type forks looked more 1970s than '60s, and indicators were standard. The new frame (shared across the range, and once again based on off-road competition experience) housed the engine oil in its top tube.

These final 250s are rare, only produced for one year, and although use of the revered Gold Star name was hated by some at the time, today they make for real period pieces.

Strengths: Faster and more revvy than a C15, snappier styling
Weaknesses: Suspect life from highly stressed engine
Value: B25 99%

1961-70 350cc singles

The 350cc B40 is thought by many to be the typical BSA unit single, but in fact it was one of the least successful when new. Only 14,000 were built, and it was outsold by the C15 by more than four

Government agencies loved the B40 – this is an Auxiliary Fire Service machine.

to one. However, the B40's survival rate appears to be better, maybe because they weren't subject to generations of sub-250 learners!

When it was launched in 1961, the B40 Star looked very similar to the C15 it was based on, but there were some significant changes. Although in a low state of tune, the 350cc engine produced a reasonable 21bhp, and the complete machine weighed only 20lb more than the C15, so performance was better, with cruising of 50-55mph, and a top speed of 75mph.

The 350cc BSA single is faster and better braked than the C15.

The crankcase was beefed up to cope with the extra power, and the B40 engine is differentiated from the C15 by virtue of its integral pushrod tunnel. It also came with bigger 18in wheels, heavier duty forks, and a bigger 7in front brake. Like the C15, the B40 was designed as a simple, reliable ride-to-work bike, though the 350 class soon dropped out of favour after the 250cc learner law came in.

There were few big changes over the B40 Star's, life though it did receive the roller-bearing big-end after only a year, and at the same time the round tank

BSA made fewer of these than the 250s, but plenty have survived.

badges were changed to BSA standard pear-shaped badges. For 1965, the contact breaker points moved to the timing cover, while clutch and kickstarter mechanisms were improved – look for engine number prefix B40F. Finally, a small number of Stars were built for the '67 model year, with the prefix B40G signifying a timing side roller main bearing – as with the C15, this is a stronger bottom end based on competition experience, and well worth seeking out.

The first variant on the B40 theme was the Sports Star SS90 launched in June 1962. It mirrored the tuning mods of the C15 SS80, with higher 8.75:1 compression ratio, larger inlet valve, stronger valve springs and a bigger carburettor. Together they added up to 24bhp at 7000rpm, enough for a top speed of 92mph, according to one contemporary road test (though most were slower). It also had the roller big-end from the start, and a close-ratio gearbox.

The SS90 looked very similar to the basic B40, apart from chrome fuel tank sides, but, for 1964, acquired sportier, slimmer mudguards, and soon after a separate chrome headlight. The US-market equivalent Sportsman SS90 was virtually identical, but with higher bars. The SS90 disappeared from the range in 1966.

An off-road B40 arrived for 1965, and, unlike the early 250cc competition bikes, the Enduro Star was a genuine dual-purpose machine, road legal with lights, horn, silencer, and brakelight. But it was no cosmetic street scrambler, with a 19in front wheel, single seat, alloy tank, no pillion rests, and a half-width 7in front brake (lighter than the road B40's full-width hub). Despite the lighting, there was no battery, and ignition was by energy transfer. The Enduro Star only lasted a year before it was replaced by the 441cc Victor.

The B40 acquired a new lease of life in 1967 when BSA was awarded a contract to supply bikes to the British Army. Just over 3000 of these WD B40s were built up to 1970, for a handful of different armed forces.

The military B40 had some important detail differences compared with the civvy street one. The frame was derived from that of the C15 competition bikes, and sported a bashplate, heavyweight two-way damped forks, and half-width front brake, reflecting the expectation that these army bikes would spend some of their time off tarmac. The engine was stronger and more softly tuned than any of its predecessors, hopefully giving a longer life in the hands of unsympathetic squaddies! It had the roller/ball-bearing main bearings and a needle-roller big-end, while a low 7:1 compression produced 18bhp. A butterfly Amal carburettor kept water and dust out better than the standard item, there was a replaceable paper oil filter, and the electrics were 12-volt, regulated by a Zener diode.

A civilian version – the B40 Rough Rider – was offered in 1968-70, aimed at Australian and New Zealand farmers, who often made use of tough and basic trail bikes to check on stock. Unlike the WD, the Rough Rider had a Concentric carburettor, full-width front hub and did without the WD's full chaincase.

Strengths: C15's traditional styling with better performance and brakes
Weaknesses: Short on glamour?
Value: B40 100%, B40 WD 144%

1965-73 441/500cc singles
The 441cc Victor was a straight development of the B40, but owed much to competition experience after Jeff Smith's two motocross world championship wins, something BSA capitalised on with the Victor Scrambles GP in 1965. The frame was based closely on that of the works bike, made of Reynolds 531 tubing and carrying the engine oil.

That was a pure competition bike, but the B44 Victor announced for 1967 took up where the B40 Enduro Star left off: a genuine dual-purpose trail bike that was road legal. The 441cc engine looked almost identical to the 350, but with a 90mm stroke to give the extra capacity and ball-bearing main bearings with a roller big-end and built-up crankshaft. It would prove to be a tough and reliable engine, in a lower state of tune than the equivalent B25, but still offering 29bhp at a less frantic 5750rpm.

Like the B40 Enduro Star it replaced, the Victor had an all-welded frame, high level exhaust, alloy fuel tank, folding footrests and battery-free electrics. For 1967, the engine gained an alloy barrel with square finning on both head and barrel, and for '68 it was given more road orientation, with battery ignition and a bigger 8in SLS front brake.

The B44 offers a good balance of performance and economy.

All BSA singles are slim, relatively lightweight bikes.

A rare B50 is worth more than any other BSA unit single.

The Victor Roadster (named Shooting Star for some markets) was launched for 1967 as a road going equivalent. It shared its frame, running gear and styling with the smaller B25, but had the same 29bhp 441cc engine as the Victor. With a top speed of over 90mph and cruising at 60-70mph, the road Victor needed better brakes, and received an 8in SLS for 1968, and BSA/Triumph's excellent twin-leading shoe 7in item for '69. There were few other changes before production ended in 1970.

The B44s were replaced by the B50 for 1971. As with the '71 B25s, these featured a new frame containing the engine oil, new conical hub brakes, and new styling and indicators. But the real change was in the bigger engine, bored out to 84mm for 498cc, and with three main bearings (not two) to strengthen the bottom end plus an improved three-stud oil pump. Power was up to 34bhp and compression a high 10:1, giving the relatively lightweight machines good performance.

There were two road variants: the purely road B50SS Gold Star, and the B50T Victor Trail, which was basically the same bike with a high level front mudguard and small 6in front brake. The B50MX was the competition variant, with the same engine but with energy transfer ignition and a racier cam. The B50SS and T lasted only until 1972, with the MX managing one more year before the whole BSA empire collapsed.

Strengths: Good performance and handling, but still lightweight
Weaknesses: Trickier to start than the small singles, B50 is expensive
Value: B44 132%, B50 225%

The Triumph singles
Triumph unit singles make an interesting footnote to the BSA unit single story, being no more than badge engineered versions of the originals, and built by BSA. The first was the TR25W, offered from 1968 as a replacement for the ageing Tiger Cub. It was really a B25 Starfire, but with some styling changes to give it more of a Triumph identity, notably a different steel fuel tank and side panels. It was given some off-

road credibility with a high-level exhaust and 19in front wheel. For 1969, it acquired the TLS front brake.

For 1971, there were Triumph versions of the BSA 250s – the T25SS Blazer and T25T Trail Blazer. As with the BSAs, the SS was the road bike, and the T a more serious trailie with high-level front mudguard, braced handlebars and alloy tank. Neither of these bikes survived into 1972.

The final Triumph single was in fact the last BSA unit single of all (unless you count CCM) – really a rebadged B50MX offered for 1974 in the USA.

CCM – BSA's extended life

BSA unit singles enjoyed an extended competition life right through the 1970s thanks to Alan Clews, who had been building BSA-based scramblers since 1972. When BSA collapsed, he bought up huge stocks of spares and carried on making beefy four-stroke motocross bikes with his own development of the familiar engine, one of which featured a four-valve head. All of them were pure competition bikes, and not road legal. Original CCMs are now collectors' machines, and fetch far higher prices than the BSAs.

The BSA single lived on through the 1970s as the CCM motocross bike.

5 Before you view
– be well informed

To avoid a wasted journey, and the disappointment of finding that the bike does not match your expectations, it will help if you're very clear about what questions you want to ask before you pick up the phone. Some of these points might appear basic, but when you're excited about the prospect of buying your dream classic, it's amazing how some of the most obvious things slip the mind. Also, check the classic bike magazine classified ads for the current values of the model you are interested in.

Where is the bike?
Is it going to be worth travelling to the next county/state, or even across a border? A locally advertised machine, although it may not sound very interesting, can add to your knowledge for very little effort, so make a visit – it might even be in better condition than expected.

Dealer or private sale
Establish early on if the bike is being sold by its owner or by a trader. A private owner should have all the history, so don't be afraid to ask detailed questions. A dealer may have more limited knowledge of the bike's history, but should have some documentation. A dealer may offer a warranty/guarantee (ask for a printed copy).

Cost of collection and delivery
A dealer may well be used to quoting for delivery. A private owner may agree to meet you halfway, but only agree to this after you have seen the bike at the vendor's address to validate the documents. Conversely, you could meet halfway and agree the sale, but insist on meeting at the vendor's address for the handover.

View – when and where?
It is always preferable to view at the vendor's home or business premises. In the case of a private sale, the bike's documentation should tally with the vendor's name and address. Arrange to view only in daylight, and avoid a wet day – the vendor may be reluctant to let you take a test ride if it's wet.

Reason for sale
Do make this one of the first questions. Why is the bike being sold and how long has it been with the current owner? How many previous owners?

Condition
Ask for an honest appraisal of the bike's condition. Ask specifically about some of the check items described in chapter 7.

All original specification
A completely original BSA will be worth more than a modified one, but certain mods (improved oil filter, electronic ignition) can also indicate a conscientious owner who has been actively riding/caring for the machine.

Matching data/legal ownership

Do frame, engine numbers and licence plate match the official registration document? Is the owner's name and address recorded in the official registration documents?

For those countries that require an annual test of roadworthiness, does the bike have a document showing it complies (an MoT certificate in the UK, which can be verified on 0845 600 5977)?

In the UK, bikes registered in 1973 or earlier are exempt from VED (Vehicle Excise Duty, better known as 'road tax'), which includes all BSA unit singles. Also in the UK, an MoT isn't compulsory for bikes built before 1960.

Does the vendor own the bike outright? Money might be owed to a finance company or bank: the bike could even be stolen. Several organisations will supply the data on ownership, based on the bike's licence plate number, for a fee. Such companies can often also tell you whether the bike has been 'written off' by an insurance company. In the UK these organisations can supply vehicle data:

HPI – 01722 422 422 – www.hpicheck.com
AA – 0870 600 0836 – www.theaa.com
RAC – 0870 533 3660 – www.rac.co.uk
Other countries will have similar organisations.

Unleaded fuel

Has the bike been modified to run on unleaded fuel?

Insurance

Check with your existing insurer before setting out – your current policy might not cover you if you do buy the bike and decide to ride it home.

How you can pay

A cheque/check will take several days to clear, and the seller may prefer to sell to a cash buyer. However, a banker's draft (a cheque issued by a bank) is as good as cash, but safer, so contact your own bank and become familiar with the formalities that are necessary to obtain one.

Buying at auction

If the intention is to buy at auction see chapter 10 for further advice.

Professional vehicle check (mechanical examination)

There are often marque/model specialists who will undertake professional examination of a vehicle on your behalf. Owners clubs may be able to put you in touch with such specialists.

6 Inspection equipment
– these items will really help

Inspection equipment
This book
Reading glasses (if you need them for close work)
Overalls
Camera/mobile phone
Compression tester
A friend, preferably a knowledgeable enthusiast

Before you rush out of the door, gather together a few items that will help as you work your way around the bike. This book is designed to be your guide at every step, so take it along and use the check boxes to help you assess each area of the bike you're interested in. Don't be afraid to let the seller see you using it.

Take your reading glasses if you need them to read documents and make close-up inspections.

Be prepared to get dirty. Take along a pair of overalls, if you have them, and a camera (though pictures taken with a mobile phone will be good enough quality), so that later you can study some areas of the bike more closely. Take a picture of any part of the bike that causes you concern, and seek a friend's opinion.

A compression tester is easy to use. It screws into the spark plug hole, easy to get to on a BSA single. With the ignition off, turn the engine over on full throttle to get the compression reading.

Ideally, have a friend or knowledgeable enthusiast accompany you: a second opinion is always valuable.

A digital camera will assist in making a record of what you see, to review later.

Some of the ideal tools to take with you: a good torch, screwdrivers, a mirror, and, of course, this guide!

www.velocebooks.com / www.veloce.co.uk
Details of all current books • New book news • Special offers

7 Fifteen minute evaluation
– walk away or stay?

Engine/frame numbers

Engine and frame numbers are mentioned several times in this book, with good reason. They are unique to the bike, a good means of checking several things: what year the bike left the factory; whether the documentation actually relates to the bike; and whether the engine and frame are original.

The engine number is located on the drive side (left-hand side) of the crankcase, just below the cylinder barrel. Numbers should be clear: any 'fuzzy' numbers could be a sign of tampering.

The engine number is easy to find and check ...

Now look for the frame number. Up to 1965, this was located on the steering head or the downtube. From 1965 to 1970 it was on the front engine mounting lug, and from '71 it moved back to the steering head. Unlike some British bikes, such as the equivalent Triumphs, the BSAs rarely had matching engine/frame numbers until 1968, from which point engines and frames were numbered together. If the engine/frame numbers don't match on a 1968 or later bike, a different engine has been fitted at some time – there may have been a good reason for this, but not having matching engine/frame numbers reduces the bike's value.

... but the frame number may be more difficult to decipher!

However, finding non-matching numbers doesn't necessarily mean it's time to walk away. The bike itself may still be an honest machine with plenty to offer – you just need to make it clear to the seller that you know it isn't 100% original and start negotiating on price.

For all bikes, check that the engine/frame number prefix confirms that the bike is the model the seller says it is. For example, it might be a standard C15 converted to look like a much rarer C15 Trials – look for the genuine 'C15T' engine number prefix. Details of all engine/frame number prefixes are in chapter 17.

Documentation

In the UK, the registration document (the V5C) lists the name and address of the bike's registered keeper. This isn't necessarily the legal owner (though it usually is), but should in any case be the person selling the bike. If any explanation for differing details doesn't ring true (eg 'I am selling it for a friend'), walk away. Also check that the engine/frame numbers on the V5C are the same as those on the bike.

An annual roadworthiness certificate – the 'MoT' in the UK – is handy proof that the bike was roadworthy when tested, but if there's a whole sheaf of them it gives evidence of the bike's history: when it was actively being used, and what the mileage was. The more of these come with the bike, the better. From 2012, bikes built before 1960 no longer required an MoT in the UK, but ask if previous MoT certificates are available.

General condition

Put the bike on its centre stand, if fitted, to shed equal light on both sides, and take a good, slow walk around it. If the owner claims it has been restored, and it has a nice shiny tank and engine cases, look more closely – how far does the 'restored' finish go? Are the nooks and crannies behind the gearbox as spotless as the fuel tank? If not, the bike may have been given a quick smarten up to sell. A generally faded look all over isn't necessarily a bad thing – it suggests a machine that hasn't been restored, and isn't trying to pretend that it has.

Put the bike on its centre stand, and have a good look around.

Now look at the engine – by far the most expensive and time-consuming thing to put right if anything's wrong. A lot of people will have told you that all old BSAs leak oil, but there shouldn't be any serious leaks if the engine is in good condition and has been put together well. It shouldn't be spattered with lube, or have oily drips underneath. Even if it's dry on top, get down on your knees and have a peek at the underside of the crankcase – nice and dry, or covered in oil? A light misting here and there is nothing to worry about, but still not inevitable.

Take the bike off the centre stand and start the engine – it should fire up within two or three kicks, and rev crisply and cleanly without showing blue or black smoke. Some top end clatter is normal, but listen for rumbles and knocks from the bottom end, and clonks from the primary drive – any of these are the precursors to serious work. While the engine's running, check that the ammeter shows the electrics are charging. If it's a B25 with an oil pressure warning light, this should have flashed off when the engine started.

Switch off the engine and put the bike back on its centre stand. Check for play in the forks, headstock and swingarm. Are there leaks from the front forks or rear shocks? Are details like the seat, badges and tank colour right for the year of the bike? (A little research helps here, and the reference books listed at the end of this volume have all this information.)

8 Key points
– where to look for problems

Are the screw or bolt heads chewed or rounded off? Is there damage to casings around bolt heads? Has someone attacked fixings with a hammer and chisel? All are sure indications of a careless previous owner with more enthusiasm than skill, coupled with a dash of youthful impatience. Not a good sign.

Are the engine and frame numbers correct for the year of the bike? Do they confirm that it's a genuine C15T or WD B40?

The frame number may be on the headstock, downtube or front engine mount. A repainted frame, as here, may make it difficult to decipher!

Minor oil leaks aren't a critical problem (though they are a bargaining point), but a serious one could suggest mechanical problems or neglect.

Listen to the engine running. Clonks or rumbles from the bottom end indicate the main or big-end bearings are worn. Excessive blue smoke means top-end wear.

Circle the Excellent (4), Good (3), Average (2) or Poor (1) box of each section as you go along. The totting up procedure is detailed at the end of the chapter. Be realistic in your marking!

Engine/frame numbers   4 3 2 1

Engine and frame numbers should be the first thing you look at – they'll tell you whether the bike really is the model it's advertised as, and on 1968-on bikes, whether the engine and frame left the factory together. That's why some BSAs are advertised with 'matching numbers,' because it means both engine and frame are original.

    The engine number is stamped on the left-hand side, just below the cylinder barrel; easy to find and to read. The figures should be clear and not 'fuzzy' – if they aren't clear, the number could have been tampered with, in which case walk away. The model code ('C15,' 'B44SS' etc) will be stamped to the left or right of the number, so check that this agrees with how the seller is describing the bike – all these model codes, with their production years, are listed in chapter 17. It's also possible to check whether the two crankcase halves are original and left the factory together. Get down on the ground and look for the bottom engine mounting bolt boss – each crankcase half has a number stamped on its half of the boss, and these should match. If not, one of the halves is not original, though that's not really a big deal if the engine's in good condition.

    Now look for the frame number, stamped on the left-hand side of the headstock or the frame downtube up to 1965, the front engine mount from that year, and the headstock from '71. This may be more difficult to read, especially if the frame has been repainted or powder coated, but it should still be visible. All the same comments apply. For 1968-on bikes, it's worth noting that if the frame and engine numbers don't match, the bike may still be honest and useable, but, being non-original, this should be reflected in the price.

    Finally, check that these numbers match those on the registration document. If they don't, it really is time to walk away.

Paint   4 3 2 1

A Triumph or Norton enthusiast would argue that BSAs were never as good-looking as these more glamorous British bikes, but the singles do have a style of their own,

Frame number is on the headstock (as here on a B50), downtube, or front engine mount.

Later engine numbers had the BSA logo stamped as a background, to make tampering more difficult.

Engine mount frame number on a B25 Starfire.

Recently repainted tank on a C15 – nicely done, and with the correct trim.

Use the reference books to find out the correct colours for the model and year.

and the paintwork was a big factor in this. The good news is that there's not that much of it: just tank, side panels and mudguards.

Many bikes had chrome or unpainted alloy mudguards, or fuel tanks sporting a large chrome panel, making a repaint easier still. Having said that, don't under-estimate the cost of a professional job, which is well worth having done, as the fuel tank in particular is such a focal point of the bike.

Look for evidence of quick and cheap resprays. Light staining around the filler cap, from spilt fuel, might polish out, but could also necessitate a respray. Generally faded original paintwork isn't necessarily a bad thing, and in fact some riders prefer this unrestored look – there are so many restored bikes around, that an honest-looking original, even if a little faded around the edges, has its own appeal.

Paint availability shouldn't be a problem, as there are often modern equivalents.

Chrome

Chrome plating is another big visual plus on these BSAs, used variously on the silencers, headlamp shell, handlebars, mirrors, and some mudguards, fuel tank panels, and other parts. The quality of the original plating is generally pretty good, though we are talking 40 or 50 years on here, so don't expect it to be pristine.

Whichever bike you're looking at, check the chrome for rust, pitting, and general dullness. Minor blemishes can be polished away, but otherwise you're looking at a replating bill. If the silencers are seriously rotted, it's a good idea to budget for a new pair – less hassle than getting the old ones replated, in any case.

Rechroming isn't cheap, but sometimes the only answer.

Tinwork

In one respect, buying a secondhand bike is far easier than purchasing a used car – there's far less bodywork to worry about. Mudguards should be straight, free of rust around the rims, and securely bolted to the bike. Styles varied, from the heavily valanced items of early C15s and B40s, to the far skimpier guards fitted to 1971-on bikes.

Shabby silencer – perfectly serviceable, but the rust should be reflected in the price.

Side panels varied, too. Rounded and usually black on C15s and B40s, while the Starfire and B44 had stylised fibreglass panels up to 1969. A simpler style came back for 1970. In all cases up to 1970, the right-hand one is (or hides) the oil tank. This should be

Examine side panels for dents and dings.

Fibreglass side panel fitted to B25 and B44 – check for cracks.

The B40 featured sensible valanced mudguards for all-year-round commuting.

Some tanks are available new – this is a B50 alloy item.

checked for leaks through the seams, as repairing entails removal and flushing out first. From '71 on, the side panels were flat (in plain black), and covers only, as the oil tank was now part of the frame. The left-hand panel covers the battery, air filter, and (if it's still there) the tool kit.

The fuel tank needs to be checked for leaks around the tap and along the seams, as well as dents and rust. Watch out for patches of filler. As with the oil tank, repairing leaks means flushing out the tank (which has to be thorough – you don't want any petrol vapour hanging about when the welding torch is fired up), but the fuel tank is at least easier to remove. Pinhole leaks can often be cured with Petseal, but anything more serious needs a proper repair. The same goes for the fibreglass tank fitted to the 1967 Starfire and Barracuda – use of ethanol in modern fuels has led to some cases of the fibreglass gradually melting, causing leaks. Ethanol can also cause steel tanks to rust, by attracting moisture. Ethanol-resistant sealants are available for steel, alloy, and glassfibre tanks – ask the seller if the bike's tank has been treated.

If the tank is beyond saving, some new ones are available, though once it's been painted, that's not a cheap option. So a very poor condition tank is a good bargaining lever.

Trim
4 3 2 1

These BSAs were not fitted with over-elaborate trim, which usually consists of just the tank badges and side panel transfers The most common fuel tank badge is the familiar BSA pear shape (circular on the early B40), either smooth and plastic coated, or cast alloy. Off-road bikes with alloy tanks had a simpler painted or transfer BSA script, as did the B40 WD and Rough Rider. Whatever the badge, it should be firmly in place, with flake-free paint. Most transfers are available new.

Tanks were fixed by a single central mounting bolt,

Starburst BSA! Tank badges like this are easily touched up.

Twin chrome trips hide the fuel tank seams, and a rubber plug covers the mounting bolt.

Most side panel transfers are available.

and this was covered by a rubber plug with a BSA logo, sometimes with one or two chrome strips to hide the tank's central seams. Road-going C15s and B40s (WD and Rough Rider apart) had rubber knee grips.

Seat

All BSA singles had a dual seat, apart from off-road bikes such as the competition C15s and B40 Enduro Star. There was a wide variation of styles, and, once again, if originality is important, you'll need to have the right one. C15s and B40s were either all-black or two-tone, off-road bikes were all black, while all B25s/B44s had an all-black seat with a racing hump for a suggestion of cafe racer. 1971-on bikes did without the hump, and grab rails were often fitted from 1968, especially to US bikes.

Cafe racer-ish humped seat on the B25/B44.

Whichever seat the bike has, the points to look for are the same. The metal pan can rust, which will eventually give way, though this is easy to check. Covers can split, which, of course, allows in rain, soaked up by the foam padding ... which never dries out. That's a recipe for a permanently wet backside, or a rock hard seat on frosty mornings (the author

Plain black seat on a C15.

Two-tone grey with white piping for a government-issue B40.

speaks from experience). New covers and complete seats in various styles are available, though recovering an old seat is a specialist job.

Rubbers

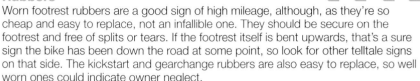

Worn footrest rubbers are a good sign of high mileage, although, as they're so cheap and easy to replace, not an infallible one. They should be secure on the footrest and free of splits or tears. If the footrest itself is bent upwards, that's a sure sign the bike has been down the road at some point, so look for other telltale signs on that side. The kickstart and gearchange rubbers are also easy to replace, so well worn ones could indicate owner neglect.

On kickstarts, beware the worn smooth rubber – your foot's liable to slip off while kicking the bike over, with painful results as the kickstart lever slams back into your leg. The rubber should also be firm on the lever and not drop off after half a dozen kicks. Of course, if the engine needs that many kicks to fire it up, then something could be wrong there anyway.

A well-worn footrest rubber, probably original.

This period replacement gearlever rubber (Britax) adds to historical interest.

Frame

There were four basic types of frame, all conventional tubular steel. All road model C15s, and B40s up to 1965, used a single front downtube and top tube branching into two smaller tubes to cradle the engine/gearbox. This was bolted to a rear subframe which supported the seat. The pre-1963 competition C15s

If you want a concours finish, frame paint like this will need a complete strip down and respray.

C15 front downtube, in good original condition.

had a modified version of this frame, with increased ground clearance and repositioned footrests.

Competition C15s from 1963 used a stronger all-welded frame, which still owed much to the original, and a development of this frame was used for the B25, B40 WD and B44. Different again was the special frame made in limited numbers for the Victor 441 Scrambles, with the oil contained in the Reynolds 531 frame tubing. Finally, all 1971-on bikes used an all-new frame, which contained the engine oil in a massive top and front downtube. This, too, was all-welded.

Whichever frame is used, if it's really shabby it will need a strip down and repaint, though as with the other paintwork, if it's original and fits in with the patina of the bike, there's a good case for leaving it as it is.

1971-on frames hold engine oil in the main tube.

Look for bent brackets, which can be heated and bent back into shape, and cracks around them, which can be welded. Those for the horn and silencer can succumb to vibration.

The most important job is to check whether the main frame is straight and true. Crash damage may have bent it, putting the wheels out of line. One way of checking is with an experienced eye, string, and a straight edge, but the surest way to ascertain a frame's straightness is on the test ride – any serious misalignment should be obvious in the way the bike handles.

Stands   4 3 2 1

All bikes were fitted with a sidestand, though most, especially the road bikes, have a centre stand as well. There aren't any particular weaknesses with either, but, of course they should be secure. When on the centre stand, the bike shouldn't wobble or lean – a sign of serious stand wear and/or imminent collapse. This affects bikes which have been started and left idling on the centre stand – all the vibration is transmitted to the ground via the stand, which doesn't do it much good.

Lights   4 3 2 1

The C15 and pre-1966 B40 had six-volt lights, with a 24/30-watt headlight which will seem dim by modern standards, even when in good condition. The 12-volt headlight fitted to everything

Stands are generally trouble-free, but check they don't wobble.

else (apart from competition and motocross bikes without any lights) was far better. Whatever the age, look out for a tarnished or

A Lucas 679 rear light, in neat alloy housing with side reflectors.

rusted reflector, which is an MoT failure, though reflectors, bulbs, glass and headlight shells are all available.

There were two styles of rear light: the Lucas 564 type fitted to the C15 and pre-1966 B40, a sort of British bike standard for the time, and the Lucas 679, with pointed rear/stop light and flat reflector. Both are available as pattern parts, though one handy modification that doesn't alter the outward appearance in any way is an LED rear/stop light bulb, available in six- or 12-volt form. This is a straight swap for the standard bulb, but won't blow, leaving you taillight-less on a dark night.

Is the headlight reflector past its best? This one's fine.

Electrics/wiring

▢4 ▢3 ▢2 ▢1

BSA unit singles used the standard British motorcycle electrics of their time. These don't have a wonderful reputation, but the 12-volt system fitted from 1967 was a great improvement. Whether six- or 12-volt systems are fitted, with good wiring, clean tight connections and electronic ignition, they can be made reliable.

The six-volt system fitted to C15s and pre-1966 B40s was fairly crude, with no automatic regulation of alternator output, so the battery was usually being either under- or over-charged. One useful feature was three settings for the ignition switch – off, on, and emergency, the latter allowing the engine to be started with a flat battery.

The 12-volt system fitted to all other road legal bikes (pure competition bikes such as the B50MX used energy transfer ignition, with no battery) had a Zener diode to prevent overcharging, and was better all round, kinder to the battery and with more power for the lights. On 1971-on bikes all electrical components (coil, Zener diode, ignition switch) were housed in an alloy box underneath the front of the fuel tank – it's very neat, but access is awkward.

So what to look for? A good general indication of the owner's

The Zener diode lives between the front forks on 1967-70 bikes.

1971-on bikes have all major electrical components in this alloy box.

attitude is the condition of the wiring – is it tidy and neat, or flopping around? The many bullet connectors need to be clean and tight, and many odd electrical problems are simply down to bad connections or a poor earth. Up to 1970, most bikes came with an

Brakelight switches can suffer from corrosion.

Is wiring neat with good connections?

ammeter, which at least gives some indication that all is well (or not) in the charging circuit.

Finally, check that everything works: lights, horn, brakelight, and indicators (fitted post '71, but sometimes removed by owners).

Wheels/tyres

All BSA unit singles used spoked wheels with chromed steel rims. Check the chrome condition on the rims – rechroming entails a complete dismantle and rebuild of the wheel. Check that none of the spokes are loose, and give each one a gentle tap with a screwdriver – any that are 'offkey' will need retensioning. If any are broken or missing, the bike is unrideable.

Tyres should have at least the legal minimum of tread – that's 1mm of tread depth across at least three-quarters of the breadth of the tyre. Beware of bikes that have been left standing (especially on the sidestand) for some time, allowing the tyres to crack and deteriorate – it's no reason to reject the bike, but a good lever to reduce the price. New tyres in suitable sizes are no problem at all.

Damaged spokes will be obvious – these are perfect.

Modern tyres are available to fit.

Wheel bearings

Wheel bearings aren't expensive, but fitting them is a hassle, and if there's play it will affect the handling. To check them, put the bike on its centre stand, put the steering on full lock, and try rocking the front wheel in a vertical plane, then spin the wheel and listen for signs of roughness. Do the same for the rear wheel. If

A wheel bearing check is easy to do.

it doesn't have a centre stand, you'll need a helper to pivot the bike on its sidestand so that a wheel is off the ground.

Steering head bearings 4 3 2 1

Again, the bearings don't cost an arm and a leg, but trouble here can affect the handling, and changing them is a big job. With the bike on the centre stand, swing the handlebars from lock to lock. They should move freely, with not a hint of roughness or stiff patches – if there is, budget for replacing them. To check for play, with the bike off the stand, put on the front brake and try gently moving the bike back and forth.

Movement at the steering head can be confused with fork wear.

Swingarm bearings 4 3 2 1

Another essential for good handling is the swingarm bearings. These should have been regularly greased, and, if they haven't, rapid wear or even seizure can result, the latter if the bike has been left standing for some time. To check for wear, get hold of the rear end of the arm on one side and try rocking the complete swing arm from side to side, relative to the frame. There should be no perceptible movement. 1966-70 bikes had Silentbloc bushes that don't need greasing.

Swingarm shouldn't have any play at all, and you'll need one hand on the frame, not the rear tyre ...

Suspension 4 3 2 1

All bikes used the same basic setup of front telescopic forks and twin rear dampers, shrouded on the C15 and pre-1966 B40 (though competition C15s had gaitered forks). The B25/B44 had gaitered forks from 1968 and for '69 added two-way shuttle damping. Rear shocks were fully exposed the same year.

From '71, Ceriani type forks with exposed stanchions were available to go with the B25/B50 new oil-bearing frame. These did a good job, but can suffer from exposure to the elements

Check both forks and rear shocks for leaks. The fork stanchions' chrome plate eventually pits, especially when exposed to the elements and/or the bike has been used in winter. When that happens, it rapidly destroys the oil seals –

Checking for fork play (steering head play may also show up on this one).

Leaks will be most obvious on exposed Ceriani-style forks (1971-on).

Evidence of a leaky fork seal on a B40.

hence the leaks. New stanchions, or reground and replated existing ones, are the answer, as there's little point in fitting new seals to rough forks.

Check for play by grabbing the bottom of the forks and trying to rock them back and forth; play here indicates worn bushes. Badly worn shocks that have lost their damping will allow a soft and bouncy ride that upsets the handling – if so, it'll be obvious on the test ride.

Instruments

Don't expect much in the way of instruments! All C15s and B40s had a small 3in Smiths speedometer built into the headlight shell, along with an ammeter. The B25/B44 had a larger separate speedo mounted on the handlebars (though still with the ammeter in the headlight shell) and '71-on bikes had a smaller speedo, with optional tachometer, while the ammeter was dropped.

Checking the speedo works obviously has to wait for the test ride – if nothing is working, the cable is the most likely culprit, but if either mileometer or speedo have ceased to function, but the other is still working, then there's something wrong internally – instrument repair is best left to a specialist. A battered and bent chrome bezel suggests that a previous owner has had a go themselves.

B25/B44 speedo, ammeter and ignition warning light.

Most bikes had an ammeter: still a useful instrument.

Full set on a B50, though a 10,000rpm rev counter is a little optimistic ...

Engine/gearbox – general impression

You can tell a lot about the likely condition of a BSA single without hearing it run. These engines are easy to work on, and the drawback of that is that it encourages keen and/or impecunious owners to take things apart themselves, often without the proper tools. So look for chewed-up screw or Allen bolt heads, and rounded off bolts, plus damage to the casings surrounding them.

It's part of motorcycling folklore that old BSAs leak oil. This isn't inevitable, and as long as the engine is in good condition and has been properly put together, it should be reasonably oil tight, but ensuring this does take some care on reassembly. Some light misting isn't a bad sign, and some leaky engines work perfectly well, though the price should reflect the appearance.

It's often difficult to find the trace of a leak, especially given the number of potential sources, such as the head gasket, cylinder base joint, primary chaincase, rockerbox, and on the C15, the pushrod tube. If the engine is generally oily, ask the owner if you can wipe it clean before the test ride – the source of any leaks should be clear after the ride. Always look underneath the engine/gearbox – they can be oil-tight up top, leaky as a sieve underneath. If oil is leaking through the gearchange shaft (kickstart on bikes with distributor ignition) then it's not the shaft at fault, but because an internal drain hole is blocked, allowing engine oil to build up in the outer case.

Many of the same comments apply to the gearbox – look for chewed fasteners and signs of neglect.

Gearbox oil dipstick on a B25/B44.

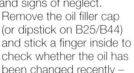

They don't *have* to leak – this C15 has covered 40,000 miles.

Remove the oil filler cap (or dipstick on B25/B44) and stick a finger inside to check whether the oil has been changed recently – nice clean EP90 ... or a frothy sludge?

If the engine still looks this pristine after the test ride, it's a good 'un.

Check underneath for oil leaks.

Engine – starting/idling

There's no getting away from the fact that four-stroke singles (especially bigger ones) do need some technique to kickstart, though it is more about that than sheer strength. This is less of an issue with the lower compression C15 and B40, and most challenging with the high compression B50.

Invariably, the owner will start the bike for you, and it's better that way because they should know what to do. The usual drill from cold is to flood the carburettor, then use the decompressor – if there is one – to give the engine a few priming kicks before easing it over top dead centre, then finally giving a good hefty kick with the decompressor off. Most engines require no throttle from cold, and some throttle when warm, but they do vary.

Is the oil returning to the tank?

Assuming correct technique, an engine in good condition should fire up within two or three kicks. The most likely culprit if it doesn't (if electronic ignition hasn't been fitted) is simply maladjusted contact breaker points and ignition timing. A more serious cause is poor compression, which indicates general wear that will need a top end rebuild to rectify. Take a compression tester along, and use it. Alternatively, the engine could just be having a fit of the sulks!

Kickstarting is more about technique than sheer strength.

Once started, the engine should idle evenly. If it sounds and feels lumpy and uneven, then contact breaker or carburettor adjustments are the most likely cause, but a knowledgeable owner should already have these spot-on. If the carburettor is worn, both new parts and complete carbs are available. Another possible cause of uneven idling and running is damage to the hoses connecting the carburettor to the air filter and inlet stub – this can cause air leaks and upset the mixture. On pre-1971 bikes, remove the oil filler cap and check that oil is returning to the tank – you should be able to see a steady stream. If it isn't, switch off immediately, as it means the oil pump isn't scavenging. If the bike hasn't been started for some time, and the oil level is suspiciously low, lube may have drained past the non-return valve and into the bottom end of the engine. The giveaway is that low level in the tank, and a lot of smoke on start-up.

The decompressor lever, where fitted, is on the bars.

Engine – smoke/noise

Air-cooled engines tend to make more mechanical noise than modern water-cooled motors, and you can expect some valve clatter even when all is well. Having said that, the C15 and B40 are quieter than the B25, B44 and B50, whose alloy cylinder barrel allows more mechanical noise than the cast iron barrel on earlier bikes.

A sign of real trouble is knocking or rumbling from the bottom end, which will

Not a BSA, but blue smoke always looks the same whichever bike it's coming from!

C15 and B40 engines should be mechanically quieter than the B25/B44/B50.

mean a complete engine rebuild for sure. Whether it's big-ends or mains that need attention, the cure is engine out and a complete strip to find out what's wrong. Beware of impressively loud megaphone silencers that may mask the more subtle knockings of a sick bottom end. Don't buy a bike that's making these noises unless it's cheap. Engine parts to cure all of this are no problem at all, for all bikes.

Bottom end life varies – the lower compression, less stressed B40 has the best chance of a long life, while the high compression high revving B25, with its plain-bearing big-end, probably the worst. The B50, with three main bearings was the strongest, and also has a much improved breather system, which reduces oil leaks. There are horror stories, but these engines can be long lived – the C15 pictured in this book had covered 40,000 miles on the original bottom end, and the B25 had just one new big-end in 25 years. For a good indication of the owner's attitude, ask how often they've changed the oil, and what they've been using – the correct answer (if a cartridge filter isn't fitted) is every 1000 miles, using 40 monograde oil.

Now look back at the silencers and blip the throttle. Blue smoke means the engine is burning oil and is a sign of general wear in the top end. That means a rebore (again, parts, including oversize pistons, are fully available) but inevitably other problems will come up once the engine is apart – the valves and guides will probably need replacing as well. Black smoke, indicating rich running, is less of a problem, caused by carburettor wear or (fingers crossed) simply a blocked air filter. Bikes without air filters should be avoided, as you don't know what nasties the motor has ingested.

Primary drive

Listen to the primary drive while the engine is running. Noises from this area – clonks or rumbles – could be one of a number of things. It could be wear in the clutch and its shock absorber, the engine sprocket chattering on worn splines or the alternator rotor coming loose on the crank's driving shaft. Of course, you won't know which without taking the primary drive cover off, but if the seller acknowledges that a noise is there, it's another good lever to reduce the price.

In theory the primary chain, running in its nice clean oil bath, should have a long life, but even here an eye needs to be kept on it. Adjustment of the chain tensioner is only possible after removing the chaincase, so this may have been neglected.

Primary chain adjustment and oil may have been neglected.

Chain/sprockets

4 3 2 1

With the engine switched off, examine the final drive chain and sprockets. Is the chain clean, well lubricated and properly adjusted? The best way to check wear is to take hold of a link and try to pull it rearwards, away from the sprocket. It should only reveal a small portion of the sprocket teeth – any more, and it needs replacing.

Check the rear sprocket teeth for wear – if they have a hooked appearance, the sprocket needs replacing. Ditto if any teeth are damaged or missing. And if the rear sprocket needs replacing, then the gearbox sprocket will too. Chain and sprockets aren't massively expensive, but changing the gearbox sprocket takes some dismantling time.

The best way to check chain wear.

Battery

4 3 2 1

Competition bikes with energy transfer ignition don't have a battery, but on all others the battery hides between the toolbox and oil tank, accessed through the left-hand side panel. Acid splashes indicate overcharging. The correct electrolyte level is a good sign of a meticulous owner, and do check that the battery is securely in place.

Engine/gearbox mountings

4 3 2 1

These need to be completely solid, with no cracks, and no missing or loose bolts – if not, the bike is not in a rideable condition. Check the front mounting (to the frame downtube), the bottom mounting (at the crankcase) and the rear mounting (rear of the gearbox).

Exhaust

4 3 2 1

A variety of exhaust systems were used, with low and high-level pipes on either side of the bike. Check that the downpipe is secure in the cylinder head (looseness causes air leaks) and examine all joints for looseness and leaks, all of which are MOT failures. The silencer should be secure, firmly mounted and in solid condition. Replacements for the various types are all available.

All mountings should be solid.

This much blueing on a downpipe is normal.

Looks solid, but is it blowing or loose?

Test ride

The test ride should be not less than 15 minutes, and you should be doing the riding – not the seller riding with you on the pillion. It's understandable that some sellers are reluctant to let a complete stranger loose on their pride and joy, but it does go with the territory of selling a bike, and, so long as you leave an article of faith (usually the vehicle you arrived in), then all should be fine. Take your driving licence in case the seller wants to see it.

Main warning lights ▢4 ▢3 ▢2 ▢1

Warning lights are notable by their absence on the C15, which doesn't have any at all! The B25/B44 had a main beam warning light, and in 1970 the B25 had an oil pressure light as well, while the 1971-on bikes added an indicator warning light. If fitted, the oil pressure light should go out immediately on the engine starting.

Engine performance ▢4 ▢3 ▢2 ▢1

Performance varies wildly, from the 15bhp C15 to the B50, which has more than twice the power and a lot more torque, but whatever the model, it should pull cleanly and without hesitation. Spitting back through the carb can be caused by the absence of an air filter, and the bike should be quite tractable at low speeds, without jerks or hesitation.

Vibration is normal, but it shouldn't be severe and hand numbing at moderate revs – certainly not below 50mph in top gear. If possible, cruise the bike at 50-60mph for five minutes, then check for oil leaks. If there's anything serious, that's a bargaining lever on price.

For all the talk of four-stroke torque, don't expect effortless acceleration from the 250s – the C15 is in a low state of tune, and the B25 only really responds to revs buzzing up to over 8000rpm. The B40, like the C15, is leisurely, though able to keep up with modern traffic, and the B44 is surprisingly quick without needing to use high revs. None of these bikes are suitable for motorways – they weren't designed to be run at constant high speed, and it's unfair to expect them to.

Clutch operation ▢4 ▢3 ▢2 ▢1

The clutch is heavier than on some modern bikes, but take-up should be smooth and positive. BSA fitted a smaller clutch than the bikes really needed (especially the bigger ones) so wear can be rapid – slip, drag, and excessive noise aren't unknown either.

Check for drag by selecting first gear from a standstill. A small crunch is normal, but a full-blooded graunch, followed by the bike trying to creep forwards, means the clutch is dragging. On the test ride, try a quick burst of hard acceleration – any clutch slip will be obvious.

1971-on bikes had a full complement of warning lights.

The only way to check engine performance – go for a ride.

The B25 should provide lively performance if worked hard.

These faults may just be down to adjustment, and if the owner is amenable, you could try adjusting at the clutch operating rod end, after first slackening right back the handlebar lever adjustment. If not, it's time to bargain on price.

Gearbox operation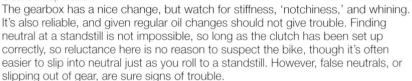

The gearbox has a nice change, but watch for stiffness, 'notchiness,' and whining. It's also reliable, and given regular oil changes should not give trouble. Finding neutral at a standstill is not impossible, so long as the clutch has been set up correctly, so reluctance here is no reason to suspect the bike, though it's often easier to slip into neutral just as you roll to a standstill. However, false neutrals, or slipping out of gear, are sure signs of trouble.

Handling

All the BSA unit singles handle well. They are relatively light and slim, with stiff suspension, easy to flick through corners, and quite agile. So any vagueness and weaving is usually down to worn forks, rear shocks, or tyres – it's not inherent. They should never feel soft and 'wallowy' – if they do, the suspension condition is your first thing to recheck. If the bike pulls to one side in a straight line, the wheels may be out of line, down to a misaligned rear wheel (easy to correct) or crash damage (a reason to reject the bike).

Brakes

All brakes are cable operated drums, and even the best ones aren't up to modern standards, though they certainly improved on later bikes. The C15's 6in cast iron drums aren't really up to fast and busy urban traffic today, but are fine for gentle cruising on quieter roads.

The B40's 7in front brake is an improvement, but better still was the 7in twin-leading shoe brake fitted to B25s and B44s for 1969, a smaller version of the respected 8in TLS brake fitted to the Triumph/ BSA 650s. 1971-on road bikes had an 8in version of the Triumph/BSA conical hub TLS front brake, and

C15 brakes are okay on quiet roads.

it's fine for the bikes' performance. Trail versions (B25T and B50T) used a much smaller 6in SLS brake, which looks marginal for modern on-road use.

Don't be alarmed if the brake lever on a TLS brake almost comes back to the bars with the bike stopped. This, and a

Twin-leading shoe front brake fitted from 1968/69 is very good.

Conical hub brakes fitted to 1971-on bikes.

generally spongey feel, are inherent, and if adjusted properly they are very powerful. Don't expect the same power from the earlier SLS brakes, but they should work smoothly and without grabbing. In this case, if the lever comes close to the bars, the brake either needs adjusting, or new shoes.

Cables

4 3 2 1

All the control cables – brakes, throttle and choke
(if fitted) – should work smoothly without stiffness or
jerking. Poorly lubricated, badly adjusted cables are an
indication of general neglect, and the same goes for
badly routed cables.

Switchgear

4 3 2 1

Like the brakes, the switchgear changed many times
over the long production run. Early machines were
simple in the extreme, with a rotary lighting/ignition
switch either low down on the tinwork between oil
tank and toolbox or in the headlamp shell, plus horn
and dipswitch buttons on the handlebars. The lighting
switch later became a toggle in the headlight shell, and
the ignition switch acquired a proper key. The 1971-on
bikes sported new Lucas alloy switches.

Whatever is fitted, check that it works positively
and reliably – the later Lucas alloy switches could let
water in, with inevitable results. Malfunctioning switches
are usually a simple problem to solve, but another
reason to bargain over price.

Cables are cheap and easy
to replace.

Early switchgear (horn/dipswitch here)
was very simple.

1971-on switchgear is very different.

Evaluation procedure

Add up the total points.

132 = excellent; 99 = good; 66 = average; 33 = poor

Bikes scoring over 92 will be completely usable and will require only maintenance
and care to preserve condition. Bikes scoring between 33 and 67 will require some
serious work (at much the same cost regardless of score). Bikes scoring between
68 and 91 will require very careful assessment of the necessary repair/restoration
costs in order to arrive at a realistic value.

10 Auctions

VICTOR 500

– sold! Another way to buy your dream

Auction pros & cons

Pros: Prices will usually be lower than those of dealers or private sellers, and you might grab a real bargain on the day. Auctioneers have usually established clear title with the seller. At the venue you can usually examine documentation relating to the bike.

Cons: You have to rely on a sketchy catalogue description of condition and history. The opportunity to inspect is limited and you cannot ride the bike. Auction machines can be a little below par and may require some work. It's easy to overbid. There will usually be a buyer's premium to pay, in addition to the auction hammer price.

Which auction?

Auctions by established auctioneers are advertised in the motorcycle magazines and on the auction houses' websites. A catalogue, or a simple printed list of the lots for auctions might only be available a day or two ahead, though often lots are listed and pictured on auctioneers' websites much earlier. Contact the auction company to ask if previous auction selling prices are available, as this is useful information (details of past sales are often available on websites).

Catalogue, entry fee and payment details

When you purchase the catalogue of the bikes in the auction, it often acts as a ticket allowing two people to attend the viewing days and the auction. Catalogue details tend to be comparatively brief, but will include information such as 'one owner from new, low mileage, full service history,' etc. It will also usually show a guide price to give you some idea of what to expect to pay and will tell you what is charged as a 'Buyer's premium'. The catalogue will also contain details of acceptable forms of payment. At the fall of the hammer an immediate deposit is usually required, the balance payable within 24 hours. If the plan is to pay by cash there may be a cash limit. Some auctions will accept payment by debit card. Sometimes credit or charge cards are acceptable, but will often incur an extra charge. A bank draft or bank transfer will have to be arranged in advance with your own bank as well as with the auction house. No bike will be released before all payments are cleared. If delays occur in payment transfers then storage costs can accrue.

Buyer's premium

A buyer's premium will be added to the hammer price: don't forget this in your calculations. It is not usual for there to be a further state tax or local tax on the purchase price and/or on the buyer's premium.

Viewing

In some instances it's possible to view on the day, or days before, as well as in the hours prior to, the auction. There are auction officials available who are willing to help out if need be. While the officials may start the engine for you, a test ride is out of the question. Crawling under and around the bike as much as you want is permitted. You can also ask to see any documentation available.

Bidding

Before you take part in the auction, decide your maximum bid – and stick to it! It may take a while for the auctioneer to reach the lot you are interested in, so use that time to observe how other bidders behave. When it's the turn of your bike, attract the auctioneer's attention and make an early bid. The auctioneer will then look to you for a reaction every time another bid is made. Usually the bids will be in fixed increments until the bidding slows, when smaller increments will often be accepted before the hammer falls. If you want to withdraw from the bidding, make sure the auctioneer understands your intentions – a vigorous shake of the head when he or she looks to you for the next bid should do the trick!

Assuming that you are the successful bidder, the auctioneer will note your card or paddle number, and from that moment on you will be responsible for the bike. If it io unoold, oithor bocauso it failed to reach the reserve or because there was little interest, it may be possible to negotiate with the owner, via the auctioneers, after the sale is over.

Successful bid

There are two more items to think about – how to get the bike home, and insurance. If you can't ride it, your own or a hired trailer is one way, another is to have it shipped using the facilities of a local company. The auction house will also have details of companies specialising in the transport of bikes.

Insurance for immediate cover can usually be purchased on site, but it may be more cost-effective to make arrangements with your own insurance company in advance, and then call to confirm the full details.

eBay & other online auctions

eBay & other online auctions once had a reputation for bargains. You could still land a BSA at a bargain price, though many traders as well as private sellers now use eBay and prices have risen. As with any auction, the final price depends how many buyers are bidding and how desperately they want the bike!

Either way, it would be foolhardy to bid without examining the bike first, which is something most vendors encourage. A useful feature of eBay is that the geographical location of the bike is shown, so you can narrow your choices to those within a realistic radius of home. Be prepared to be outbid in the last few moments of the auction. Remember, your bid is binding and that it will be very, very difficult to get restitution in the case of a crooked vendor fleecing you – caveat emptor! Look at the seller's rating as well as the bike.

Be aware that some bikes offered for sale in online auctions are 'ghost' machines. Don't part with any cash without being sure that the vehicle does actually exist and is as described (usually pre-bidding inspection is possible).

Auctioneers

Bonhams www.bonhams.com
Cheffins www.cheffins.co.uk
eBay www.ebay.com
H&H www.classic-auctions.co.uk
Shannons www.shannons.com.au
Silver www.silverauctions.com

11 Paperwork

The paper trail

Classic bikes sometimes come with a large portfolio of paperwork accumulated and passed on by a succession of proud owners. This documentation represents the real history of the machine, from which you can deduce how well it's been cared for, how much it's been used, which specialists have worked on it and the dates of major repairs and restorations. All of this information will be priceless to you as the new owner, so be very wary of bikes with little paperwork to support their claimed history.

Registration documents

All countries/states have some form of registration for private vehicles, whether it's like the American 'pink slip' system or the British 'log book' system.

It is essential to check that the registration document is genuine, that it relates to the bike in question, and that all the details are correctly recorded, including frame and engine numbers (if these are shown). If you are buying from the previous owner, his or her name and address will be recorded in the document: this will not be the case if you are buying from a dealer.

In the UK the current (Euro-aligned) registration document is the V5C, and is printed in coloured sections of blue, green and pink. The blue section relates to the motorcycle specification, the green section has details of the registered keeper (who is not necessarily the legal owner), and the pink section is sent to the DVLA in the UK when the bike is sold. A small section in yellow deals with selling within the motor trade.

In the UK, the DVLA will provide details of earlier keepers of the bike upon payment of a small fee, and much can be learned in this way.

If the bike has a foreign registration, there may be expensive and time-consuming formalities to complete. Do you really want the hassle? More recently, BSAs exported to the USA have been re-imported to the UK. It sounds like a great chance to buy a bike that has only been used on dry, West Coast roads, with the added glamour of US heritage. However, you'll have to buy the bike sight unseen, and the paperwork involved in importing and re-registering is a daunting prospect. That means employing a shipping agent; you'll also have to budget in the shipping costs. Then there's the 6% (at the time of writing) import duty on the bike and shipping costs, then 20% VAT on the whole lot. Unless you're after a rare US-only spec bike, it's not worth the hassle.

Roadworthiness certificate

Most country/state administrations require that bikes are regularly tested to prove they are safe for use on the public highway. In the UK, that test (the 'MoT') is carried out at approved testing stations, for a fee. In the USA the requirement varies, but most states insist on an emissions test every two years as a minimum, while the police are charged with pulling over unsafe-looking vehicles.

In the UK the test is required annually for all post-1960 vehicles over three years old. Even if it isn't a legal necessity, a conscientious owner can opt to put the bike through the test anyway, as a health check. Of particular relevance for older bikes is that the certificate issued includes the mileage reading recorded at the test date, and, therefore, becomes an independent record of that machine's history. Ask the seller if previous certificates are available. Without an MoT, the bike should be trailered to its new home, unless you insist that a valid MoT is part of the deal. (Not such a bad idea this, as at least you will know the bike was roadworthy on the day it was tested, and you don't need to wait for the old certificate to expire before having the test done.)

Road licence

The administration of every country/state charges some kind of tax for the use of its road system, with the actual form of the 'road licence' and how it is displayed varying enormously country to country and state to state.

Whatever the form of the road licence, it must relate to the vehicle carrying it, and must be present and valid if the bike is to be ridden on the public highway legally. The value of the license will depend on the length of time it will continue to be valid.

In the UK if a bike is untaxed because it has not been used for a period of time, the owner has to inform the licencing authorities, otherwise the vehicle's date-related registration number will be lost and there will be a painful amount of paperwork to get it re-registered. As mentioned previously, all BSA singles are old enough to be exempt from road tax in the UK, and from October 2014 they (along with everything else) were not required to display a paper tax disc.

Certificates of authenticity

For many makes of classic bike it is possible to get a certificate proving the age and authenticity (eg engine and frame numbers, paint colour and trim) of a particular machine. These are sometimes called 'heritage certificates' and if the bike comes with one of these it is a definite bonus. If you want to obtain one, the owners club is the best starting point – contact details are in chapter 16.

Valuation certificate

Hopefully, the vendor will have a recent valuation certificate, or letter signed by a recognised expert stating how much he, or she, believes the particular bike to be worth (such documents, together with photos, are usually needed to get 'agreed value' insurance). Generally such documents should act only as confirmation of your own assessment of the bike rather than a guarantee of value, as the expert has probably not seen it in the flesh. The easiest way to find out how to obtain a formal valuation is to contact the owners' club.

Service history

Usually these bikes will have been serviced at home by enthusiastic (and hopefully capable) owners for a good number of years. Nevertheless, try to obtain as much service history and other paperwork pertaining to the bike as you can. Naturally specialist garage receipts score most points in the value stakes. However, anything helps in the great authenticity game: items like the original bill of sale, handbook, parts invoices and repair bills, adding to the story and the character of the machine. Even a brochure correct to the year of the bike's manufacture is a useful document and something that you could well have to search hard to locate in future years. If the seller claims that the bike has been restored, then expect receipts and other evidence from a specialist restorer.

If the seller claims to have carried out regular servicing, ask what work was completed, when, and seek some evidence of it being carried out. Your assessment of the bike's overall condition should tell you whether the seller's claims are genuine.

Restoration photographs

If the seller tells you that the bike has been restored, then expect to be shown a series of photographs taken while the restoration was under way. Pictures taken at various stages, and from various angles, should help you gauge the thoroughness of the work. If you buy the bike, ask if you can have copies of all the photographs, as they form an important part of its history.

12 What's it worth?
– let your head rule your heart

Condition
If the bike you've been looking at is really ratty, you've probably not bothered to use the marking system in chapter 9 – 30 minute evaluation. You may not have even got as far as using that chapter at all!

If you did use the marking system in chapter 9 you'll know whether the bike is in Excellent (maybe Concours), Good, Average or Poor condition or, perhaps, somewhere in between these categories.

To keep up to date with prices, buy the latest editions of the classic bike magazines and check the classified and dealer ads, both in the magazines and online – these are particularly useful, as they enable you to compare private and dealer prices. Most of the magazines run auction reports as well, which publish the actual selling prices, as do the auction house websites. Remember that the price listed for online auctions (unless it's a 'Buy it Now' price) is only the highest current bid, not the final selling price.

BSA singles are less sought after than the equivalent Triumphs, so prices tend to be lower. But there is a significant difference in price between models. In general C15s remain the most affordable, followed by B40s and B25s (with the rarer C15T, C15S, SS80 and SS90 variants inevitably worth more). B44s fetch a little more still, and the rare B50 is the most expensive BSA single of all.

Bear in mind that a bike that is truly a recent show winner could be worth more than the highest price usually seen. Assuming that the bike you have in mind is not in show/concours condition, then relate the level of condition that you judge it to be in with the appropriate price in the adverts. How does the figure compare with the asking price?

Before you start haggling with the seller, consider what affect any variation from standard specification might have on the bike's value. This is a personal thing: for some, absolute originality is non-negotiable, while others see non-standard parts as an opportunity to pick up a bargain. Do your research in the reference books, so that you know the bike's spec when it left the factory. That way, you shouldn't end up paying a top-dollar price for a non-original bike. If you are buying from a dealer, remember prices are generally higher than in private sales.

Striking a deal
Negotiate on the basis of your condition assessment, mileage, and fault rectification cost. Also take into account the bike's specification. Be realistic about the value, but don't be completely intractable: a small compromise on the part of the vendor or buyer will often facilitate a deal at little real cost.

13 Do you really want to restore?
– it'll take longer and cost more than you think

There's a romance about restoration projects, about bringing a sick bike back to blooming health, and it's tempting to buy something that 'just needs a few small jobs' to bring it up to scratch. But there are two things to think about: one, once you've got the bike home and begun taking it apart, those few small jobs could turn into big ones. Two, restoration takes time, which is a precious thing in itself. Be honest with yourself – will you get as much pleasure from working on the bike as you would from riding it?

If the bike's incomplete, this will slow the restoration.

Of course, you could hand over the whole lot to a professional, and the biggest cost involved there is not the new parts, but the sheer labour involved. Such restorations don't come cheap, and if taking this route there are four other issues to bear in mind as well.

First, make it absolutely clear what you want doing. Do you want the bike to be 100% original at the end of the process, or simply useable? Do you want a concours finish, or are you prepared to put up with a few blemishes on the original parts?

Second, make sure that not only is a detailed estimate involved, but that it is more or less binding. There are too many stories of a person being quoted one figure, only to be presented with an invoice for a far larger one!

Third, check that the company you're dealing with has a good reputation. The owners' club, or one of the reputable parts suppliers, should be able to make a few recommendations.

Rusty chrome, but otherwise everything's there on this B25SS.

Finally, having a BSA professionally restored is unlikely to make financial sense, as it will probably cost more than the finished bike will be worth. Not that this should put you off, if you have the budget, and really want to do it this way.

Restoring the bike yourself requires a number of skills, which is fine if you already have them, but if you haven't it's good not to make your newly acquired bike part of the learning curve! Can you weld? Are you confident about rebuilding

Minor oil leaks are unsightly, but the bike will run perfectly well.

Are you prepared to put up with minor blemishes?

an engine? Do you have a warm, well-lit garage with a solid workbench and good selection of tools?

Be prepared for a top-notch professional to put you on a lengthy waiting list, or, if tackling a restoration yourself, expect things to go wrong, and set aside extra time to complete the task. Restorations can stretch into years when things like life intrude, so it's good to have some sort of target date.

There's a lot to be said for a rolling restoration, especially as the summers begin to pass with your bike still off the road. This is not the way to achieve a concours finish, which can only really be achieved via a thorough nut-and-bolt rebuild, without the bike getting wet, gritty, and salty in the meantime, but an 'on-the-go' restoration does have its plus points. Riding helps maintain your interest as the bike's condition improves, and it's also more affordable than trying to do everything in one go. In the long run, it will take longer, but you'll get some on-road fun out of the bike in the meantime.

14 Paint problems
– bad complexion, including dimples, pimples and bubbles

Paint faults generally occur due to lack of protection/maintenance, or to poor preparation prior to a respray or touch-up. Some of the following conditions may be present in the bike you're looking at:

Orange peel
This appears as an uneven paint surface, similar to the appearance of the skin of an orange. The fault is caused by the failure of atomised paint droplets to flow into each other when they hit the surface. It's sometimes possible to rub out the effect with proprietary paint cutting/rubbing compound or very fine grades of abrasive paper. A respray may be necessary in severe cases. Consult a paint shop for advice.

Cracking will eventually spread.

Cracking
Severe cases are likely to have been caused by too heavy an application of paint (or filler beneath the paint). Also, insufficient stirring of the paint before application can lead to the components being improperly mixed, and cracking can result. Incompatibility with the paint already on the panel can have a similar effect. To rectify it is necessary to rub down to a smooth, sound finish before respraying the problem area.

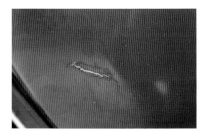

Quickly touched-up scratches are obvious.

Crazing
Sometimes the paint takes on a crazed rather than a cracked appearance when the problems mentioned under 'cracking' are present. This problem can also be caused by a reaction between the underlying surface and the paint. Paint removal and respraying the problem area is usually the only solution.

Blistering
Almost always caused by corrosion of the metal beneath the paint. Usually perforation will be found in the metal and the damage will often be worse than that suggested by the area of blistering. The metal will have to be repaired before repainting.

If there's rust underneath the paint, it will always find a way through.

Micro blistering

Usually the result of an economy respray, where inadequate heating has allowed moisture to settle on the vehicle before spraying. Consult a paint specialist, but damaged paint will have to be removed before partial or full respraying. Can also be caused by bike covers that don't 'breathe.'

Fuel stains like this can usually be polished out.

Fading

Some colours, especially reds, are prone to fading if subject to strong sunlight for long periods without the benefit of polish protection. Sometimes proprietary paint restorers and/or paint cutting/rubbing compounds will retrieve the situation, but often a respray is the only real solution.

Peeling

Often a problem with metallic paintwork when the sealing lacquer becomes damaged and begins to peel off. Poorly applied paint may also peel. The remedy is to strip and start again.

Dimples

Dimples in the paintwork are caused by the residue of polish (particularly silicone types) not being removed properly before respraying. Paint removal and repainting is the only solution.

15 Problems due to lack of use

– just like their owners, BSAs need exercise!

Like any piece of engineering, and indeed like human beings, BSA singles deteriorate if they sit doing nothing for long periods. This is especially relevant if the bike is laid up for six months of the year, as some are.

Rust
If the bike is put away wet, and/or stored in a cold, damp garage, the paint, metal and brightwork will suffer. Ensure the machine is completely dry and clean before going into storage, and, if you can afford it, invest in a dehumidifier to keep the garage atmosphere dry.

Seized components
Swingarm bearings, forks and brake parts can all seize, given enough time and some moisture. Cables are vulnerable to seizure, too – the answer is to thoroughly lube them beforehand, and come into the garage to give them a couple of pulls once a week or so.

Even partially dismantled bikes need looking after.

Give the levers a pull once a week.

Tyres

If the bike's been left on its side stand, most of its weight is on the tyres, which will develop flat spots and cracks over time. Always leave the bike on its centre stand, which takes weight off the tyres.

Engine

Old, acidic oil can corrode bearings. Many riders change the oil in the spring before putting the bike back on the road, but really it should be changed just before the bike is laid up, so that the bearings are sitting in fresh oil. The same goes for the gearbox. While you're giving the cables their weekly exercise, turn the engine over slowly on the kickstart with the ignition off. Don't start it though – running the engine for a short time does more harm than good, as it produces a lot of moisture internally, which the engine doesn't get hot enough to burn off. That will attack the engine internals and the silencers.

Battery/electrics

Either remove the battery and give it a top-up charge every couple of weeks, or connect it to a battery top-up device such as the Optimate, which will keep it

Don't leave it there too long – it was built to be ridden ...

permanently fully charged. Damp conditions will allow fuses and earth connections to corrode, creating electrical troubles for the spring. Eventually, wiring insulation will harden and fail.

16 The Community

– key people, organisations and companies in the BSA world

Auctioneers
Bonhams – www.bonhams.com
Cheffins – www.cheffins.co.uk
eBay – www.ebay.com
H&H – www.classic-auctions.co.uk
Shannons – www.shannons.com.au
Silver – www.silverauctions.com

Clubs across the world
BSA Owners Club – UK
www.bsaownersclub.co.uk

Austria
Email: Martin.Prinoth@soplar.ch

Australia
www.bsa.asn.au

Belgium
Email: dirvere@skynet.be

Canada
Email: mears43@hotmail.com

Denmark
www.bsa.dk

France
Thierry Berthelot, 14 Rue de la Place St German, 17400 Varaise, France

Germany
Email: DieterBuettner@gmx.net

Indonesia
www.bsaoi.org

Netherlands
www.bsa-oc.com

New Zealand
www.bsa.org.nz

Norway
Email: p-braat@online.no

Specialists

There are many BSA specialists all over the world, and we have restricted our listing to UK companies, with one exception. This list does not imply recommendation, and is not deemed to be comprehensive.

Alpha Bearings
Roller bearing conversion (C15, B40)
www.alpha-bearings.com – tel: 01384 255151

Britbits
Spares – Bournemouth
www.britbits.co.uk – tel: 01202 483675

BSA Unit Singles LLC
Spares – Jaffrey, NH, USA
www.bsaunitsingles.com – tel: +001 978 829 2500

Burton Bike Bits
Spares – Staffordshire
www.burtonbikebits.net – tel: 01530 564362

C and D Autos
Spares – West Midlands
www.canddautos.co.uk – tel: 01564 795000

Classic Motorcycle Spares
Spares – Wiltshire
www.classicmotorcyclespares.com – tel: 01793 295014

Electrex World
Ignition/electrical parts
www.electrexworld.co.uk – tel: 01491 682369

Hawkshaw Motorcycles
Spares – Liverpool
www.hawkshawmotorcycles.com – tel: 0151 949 0991

Lightning Spares
Spares – Cheshire
www.lightning-spares.co.uk – tel: 0161 969 3850

MS Motorcycles
Paint and dating service
www.msmotorcyclesuk.com – tel: 07773 296826

Robin James Engineering
Restorations – Herefordshire
www.robinjamesengineering.com – tel: 01568 612800

SRM Engineering
Spares/engineering – Aberystwyth
www.srm-engineering.com – tel: 01970 627771

Thunderbird Spares
Spares – Lancashire
www.thunderbirdspares.com
email spares@thunderbirdspares.co.uk

Unity Equipe
Spares – Lancashire
www.unityequipe.com – tel: 01706 632237

Books and websites
Some of these books are out of print, but still available online.

The Rupert Ratio Unit Single Engine Manual, Rupert Ratio, Panther Publishing 2003
The Rupert Ratio Unit Single Manual Volume 2, Rupert Ratio, Panther Publishing
  2014 (Both Ratio books essential reading once you've bought a BSA single.)
BSA Singles Restoration, Roy Bacon, Andover Norton International, republished
  2012
BSA Unit Singles: The Complete Story, Matthew Vale, Crowood
British Motorcycles Since 1950 Vol 2, Steve Wilson, PSL 1992
BSA Motorcycles - The Final Evolution, Brad Jones, Veloce Publishing 2014
BSA Singles Gold Portfolio 1945-63, RM Clarke, Brooklands Books
BSA Singles Gold Portfolio 1964-74, RM Clarke, Brooklands Books

www.b50.org – lots of information on the B50.
www.bsawdb40.com – ditto for the WD B40.

17 Vital statistics

– essential data at your fingertips

Listing the vital statistics of every BSA unit single variant would take far more room than we have here, so I've picked three representative models: the 1959 C15 Star, 1965 B40 Star, and 1970 B44 Shooting Star.

Max speed
1959 C15: 70mph
1965 B40: 75mph
1970 B44: 88mph

Engine
1959 C15: Air-cooled single, 247cc, bore x stroke 67 x 70mm
Compression ratio 7.5:1, 15bhp @ 7000rpm
1965 B40: Air-cooled single, 343cc, bore x stroke 79 x 70mm
Compression ratio 7.0:1, 21bhp @ 7000rpm
1970 B44: Air-cooled single, 441cc, bore x stroke 79 x 90mm
Compression ratio 9.4:1, 29bhp @ 5750rpm

Gearbox
1959 C15: Four-speed, 1st 15.96:1, 2nd 10.54:1, 3rd 7.65:1, 4th 5.98:1
1965 B40: Four-speed, 1st 12.3:1, 2nd 9.65:1, 3rd 7.0:1, 4th 5.48:1
1970 B44: Four-speed, 1st 14.2:1, 2nd 8.84:1, 6.70:1, 4th 5.36:1

Brakes
1959 C15: Front 6in single-leading shoe, rear 6in single-leading shoe
1965 B40: Front 7in single-leading shoe, rear 6in single-leading shoe
1970 B44: Front 7in twin-leading shoe, rear 6in single-leading shoe

Electrics
1959 C15: 6-volt, alternator
1965 B40: 6-volt, alternator
1970 B44: 12-volt, alternator

Weight
1959 C15: 280lb
1965 B40: 300lb
1970 B44: 320lb

Major change points by model years
1958: C15 launched
1959: C15 Trials and Scrambles launched
1961: C15 SS80 and B40 Star launched
1962: Roller bearing big-end (B40), SS90 launched
1963: All-welded frame (C15T & S)

1964: Roller bearing big-end (C15)
1965: CB points move to timing case (all), B40 Enduro Star launched
1966: Roller/ball-bearing crank (C15), Sportsman replaces SS80, B44 Victor GP & Enduro launched
1967: C25 Barracuda, B25 Starfire, B40 WD, B44 Roadster/Shooting Star launched
1968: B40 Rough Rider launched, 8in SLS front brake (B44)
1969: Improved forks and TLS front brake (B25, B44), B25 Fleetstar launched
1971: Whole range renewed. B25/B50 Gold Star & Victor Trail launched
1973: Final B50 MX built

Engine/frame numbers

Production for each model year began in August. That is, 1967 model bikes began rolling off the lines in August 1966, after the summer holidays. Numbers refer to the first engine/frame built of each model in each model year.

1959	Engine	Frame
C15 Star	C15 101	C15 101
C15 Scrambles	C15S 101	C15S 101
C15 Trials	C15T 101	C15S 101

1960	Engine	Frame
C15 Star	C15 11001	C15 11001
C15 Scrambles	C15S 301	C15S 501
C15 Trials	C15T 301	C15S 501

1961	Engine	Frame
C15 Star	C15 21251	C15 22001
C15 Sports Star 80	C15SS 101	C15 22001
C15 Scrambles	C15S 2112	C15S 2701
C15 Trials	C15T 101	C15S 2701
B40 Star	B40 101	B40 101

1962	Engine	Frame
C15 Star	C15 29839	C15 31801
C15 Sports Star 80	C15SS 1101	C15 31801
C15 Scrambles	C15S 3101	C15S 3558
C15 Trials	C15T 1451	C15S 3558
B40 Star	B40 3601	B40 3511
B40 Sports Star 90	B40BSS 101	B40 3511

1963	Engine	Frame
C15 Star	C15 41807	C15 38035
C15 Police	C15P 41807	C15 38035
C15 Sports Star 80	C15SS 2705	C15 38035
C15 Scrambles	C15C 4001	C15C 101
C15 Star America	C15B 409	C15 38035
C15 Starfire Roadster	C15SR 101	C15C 101
C15 Trials	C15T 2001	C15C 101
C15 Trials Pastoral	C15T 1602	C15C 101

B40 Star	B40 4506	B40 5017
B40 Sports Star 90	B40SS 180	B40 5017
B40 Star USA	B40B 563	B40 5017

1964	Engine	Frame
C15 Star	C15D 101	C15 4211
C15 Sports Star 80	C15SS 3633	C15 4211
C15 Police	C15DP 101	C15 4211
C15 Star America	C15DB 101	C15 4211
C15 Scrambles	C15S 4373	C15C 853
C15 Starfire Roadster	C15SR 225	C15C 853
C15 Trials	C15T 2116	C15C 853
C15 Trials Pastoral	C15T 2116	C15E 101
B40 Star	B40 5275	B40 6668
B40 Police	B40P 5275	B40 6668
B40 Super Star USA	B40B 1088	B40 6668
B40 Sports Star 90	B40SS 426	B40 6668
B40 Enduro Star USA	B40T 143	C15C 1601

1965	Engine	Frame
C15 Star	C15F 101	C15 45501
C15 Star America	C15FB 101	C15 45501
C15 Police	C15FP 101	C15 45501
C15 Sports Star 80	C15FSS 101	C15 45501
C15 Scrambles	C15FS 101	C15C 1601
C15 Starfire Roadster	C15FSR 101	C15C 1601
C15 Trials	C15FT 101	C15C 1601
C15 Trials Cat	C15FT 101	C15C 1601
B40 Star	B40F 101	B40 7775
B40 Police	B40FP 101	B40 7775
B40 Sports Star 90	B40FSS 101	B40 7775
B49 Sportsman USA	B40FB 101	B40 7775
B40 Enduro Star	B40FE 101	C15C 1601

1966	Engine	Frame
C15 Star	C15F 2089	C15 49001
C15 Sportsman	C15FSS 2001	C15 49001
B40 Star	B40F 1149	B40 9937
B40 Star (mod engine)	B40G 101	B40 9973
B44 Victor Grand Prix	B44 101	B44 101
B44 Enduro	B44E 101	B44E 3137

1967	Engine	Frame
C15 Star	C15G 101	C15G 101
C15 Police	C15PG 101	C15PG 101
C15 Sportsman	C15SG 101	C15SG 101
B25 Starfire USA	C25 101	C25 101
C25 Barracuda	C25 101	C25 101
B40 Star	B40G 201	B40G 201

	Engine	Frame
B40 Military	B40GB 101	B40GB 101
B40 Military Australia	B40GA 101	B40GA 101
B44 Victor Grand Prix	B44 131	B44 267
B44 Victor Enduro	B44EA 101	B44EA 101
B44 Victor Roadster	B44R 101	B44R 101

1968	Engine	Frame
B25 Starfire	B25B 101	B25B 101
B25 Fleetstar	B25FS 101	B25FS 101
B40 Military	B40M 101	B40M 101
B40 Military Danish	B40GD 101	B40GD 101
B44 Shooting Star	B44B 101	B44B 101SS
B44 Victor Special	B44B 101	B44B 101VS

From 1969, the prefix model letters (eg B44SS) became the suffix. The new two-letter prefix denote the month and year the bike was built. Eg ED 12345 B44SS would be a B44SS built in May 1970. Also, engine and frame numbers should match from 1969, though some sources put this change at 1966.

Month	Model year
A January	C 1969
B February	D 1970
C March	E 1971
D April	G 1972
E May	H 1973
G June	J 1974
H July	
J August	
K September	
N October	
P November	
X December	

1969	Engine	Frame
B25 Starfire	B25S 101	B25S 101
B25 Fleetstar	B25FS 101	B25FS 101
B40 Military	B40GR 201	B40GR 201
B40 Military (Army)	B40GB 3001	B40GB 3001
B40 Military (Navy)	B40GN 101	B40GN 101
B40 Military Danish	B40GD 750	B40WD 750
B40 Rough Rider	HCB40 462	HCB40 462M
B44 Shooting Star	B44SS 101	B44SS 101
B44 Victor Special	B44VS 101	B44VS 101

1970	Engine	Frame
B25 Starfire	B25S 101	B25S 101
B25 Fleetstar	B25FS 101	B25FS 101
B40 Military Danish	B40GD 1001	B40GD 1001

B44 Shooting Star	B44SS 101	B44SS 101
B44 Victor Special	B44VS 101	B44VS 101

1971	Engine	Frame
B25 Gold Star SS	B25SS 101	B25SS 101
B25 Fleet Star	B25FS 101	B25FS 101
B25 Victor Trail	B25T 101	B25T 101
B50 Gold Star SS	B50SS 101	B50SS 101
B50 Victor Trail	B50T 101	B50T 101
B50 Moto Cross	B50MX 101	B50MX 101

1972	Engine	Frame
B50 Gold Star SS	B50SS 101	B50SS 101
B50 Victor Trail	B50T 101	B50T 101
B50 Moto Cross	B50MX 101	B50MX 101

1973	Engine	Frame
B50 Moto Cross	B50MX 101	B50MX 101

www.velocebooks.com / www.veloce.co.uk
Details of all current books • New book news • Special offers

The Essential Buyer's Guide™ series ...

978-1-845840-22-8

978-1-845840-26-6

978-1-845840-29-7

978-1-845840-77-8

978-1-845840-99-0

978-1-904788-70-6

978-1-845841-01-0

978-1-845841-19-5

978-1-845841-13-3

978-1-845841-35-5

978-1-845841-36-2

978-1-845841-38-6

978-1-845841-46-1

978-1-845841-47-8

978-1-845841-63-8

978-1-845841-65-2

978-1-845841-88-1

978-1-845841-92-8

978-1-845842-00-0

978-1-845842-04-8

978-1-845842-05-5

978-1-845842-70-3

978-1-845842-81-9

978-1-845842-83-3

978-1-845842-84-0

978-1-845842-87-1

978-1-84584-134-8

978-1-845843-03-8

978-1-845843-09-0

978-1-845843-16-8

978-1-845843-29-8

978-1-845843-30-4

978-1-845843-34-2

978-1-845843-38-0

978-1-845843-39-7

978-1-845841-61-4

978-1-845842-31-4

978-1-845843-07-6

978-1-845843-40-3

978-1-845843-48-9

978-1-845843-63-2

978-1-845844-09-7

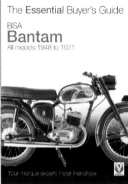

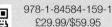
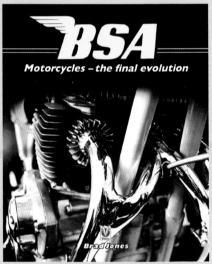

The *Off-Road Giants!* series

Three volumes of fascinating and nostalgic rider profiles from the '50s, '60s and '70s, covering legends such as Badger Watts, Dave Bickers and Olga Kevelos. Featuring hundreds of period photographs, these books beautifully capture a much-loved time in motorsport.

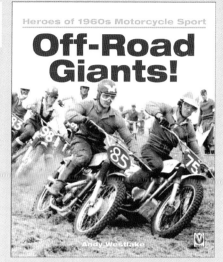

ISBN: 978-1-845845-89-6
eBook only • Flowing layout • Base price
£14.99 • 115 pictures

ISBN: 978-1-845843-23-6
Hardback • 25x20.7cm • £19.99*
UK/$39.95* USA • 128 pages
• 123 b&w pictures

ISBN: 978-1-845847-45-6
Hardback • 25x20.7cm • £25* UK/$45* USA
• 128 pages • 124 b&w pictures

Index